# Midnight Solace

poems

Sin Dee

Copyright © 2021 Sin Dee

*to each and everyone of you ...*

*where there is hope, all things are possible ...*

The love
of poetry
is truly an
acquired taste.

Just like a
fine wine
aged to
perfection
through
wisdom
and knowledge.

Relax
and enjoy
the flavor
of every word!

As the last
flame
from
the burning
candle
died,
so too
did my
desire to
foolishly
continue
to wait
on
someone
who
no longer
cares
to join me.

- get over it, move on.

Once
upon a time
there was this
great author …

She believed
she could write,

and so she did.

First …

love
yourself,

above
all
others!

Learn to
truly
love yourself.

Only then
will you be free
to love
another.

Around
every corner
there's
a new memory,

just waiting
to be made!

Love your life today
live like there's no tomorrow
laugh at yesterday!

Start small
aim high
Dream big!

I love you
even
when I hate you.

As far as
the moon,
the stars
and everything
in between.

Today
is a perfect day
to wipe the slate clean
and start all over ...

Be kind to all
sit back,
put your feet up,
feel the happiness
from within
shining through!

Everybody
has a chapter
in life
they'd prefer
to keep
to themselves.

It's those
hidden chapters
that make us
who we are!

Life is like
a mystery novel
just waiting
for the next chapter
to be written …

If a mistake
is made
simply tear out
the page,

and　　　　start　　　　again　　　　…

As one door
closes,

there's a whole
universe
full of opportunity
waiting,

behind another.

Hold on to
your
best friends.

A good friend
knows the poem …

A best friend
helped you
compose it!

Born to write …

Never to be seen
without
her pen
and notepad
in hand.

Yet to be written ...

Love is …
Finding that
perfect someone
to spend eternity with …
                    *YOU!*

In times
of writer's block,
remember ...

Every great
book ...

Started out as
a blank page!

If it has
already
been written
in the stars ...

Why not
sign it in stone
instead?

It takes
a special kind
of person
to enjoy poetry ...

I guess
you and I
must be
pretty special.

No, we are awesome!

Write, write, write,

If at first ...

You don't succeed
drink more coffee,

and write again ...

Coffee is a

*blessing*

sent straight
from above.

Drink and get hyper
enjoy an all nighter.

When ...

You are tired
of staring at
those same old
family photos
still hanging on
your wall ...

Here's a
temporary fix ...

Replace all
old photos
with cats!

Any cats will do,
the crazier
the better.

And voila,
problem solved!

*CATS*

are
the
perfect
companions
who
will
always
love
you
even
on
days
when
you
don't
seem
to
love
yourself.

.

*WORDS ...*

are
the cheapest
form
of pleasure!

*And*

                                                  *with*

                   *this*

                                *pen,*

*I*                                                         *thee*

             *write ...*

If ...

you're gonna
love me,

Love me for

*ALL*

of me,

flaws included!

Coffee
and a good
Book

 = 's

true
happiness!

Behind
every
great book,
there's
an even
greater author,

Just waiting
to share
their story
with
the world!

I too ...
have lived through
life's battles ...

Leaving
many scars,

That

*ONLY*

add to
my character!

Some poets
write of
starry nights
and dreams
that shine
and glitter.

This poet
writes of a
handsome man
who's all
she's ever
wished for!

Life is
short so ...
make it count!

Reach
further then
every single star!

No goal
you reach for
is ever unattainable!

Be
true
to
yourself
and
always
believe
with
honesty ...

You're
sure
to
succeed!

My
favorite
part of

*ME*

is
the pieces
of

*YOU*

I've
saved
inside
my heart.

Write more,

worry less!

Good night
world ...

Good morning
emptiness ...

You
were
up and
gone before
daylight
ever stood
a chance!

She dreamt
of all the things
she could
accomplish
and so she did ...

Follow those
dreams ...

Wherever
they
may lead you.

Everyone
had to
start out
somewhere!

In times of
uncertainty

Remember ...

A smile
can be seen
from behind
your mask.

What an extremely
boooooooooring
world this would be,

If ...

we were all
the same.

Be strange,
be different,
be unique,

just be you.

Love
who you are.

Love
where you're at.

Love
who you're with.

Love ...

All that is Life!

Always
surround
yourself
with
the
people
who
can
make
you
laugh
at
absolutely
nothing!

Remember
to
enjoy
the beauty
in bold
colors
of a rainbow,

after the
storm has
subsided.

When
the
waves
get
too
rough
simply
float
on
your
back
and
drift
ashore.

The average
teen girl
is a little bit of this
or a little bit of that,
pizza or poutine
straightened or curled
make up or elle natural
lashes or not
Disney or Netflix
homeschool or highschool
drama or none,

Just some
of the many
difficult decisions
a teen girl
must endure.

Snowflakes
have
a
magical
way
of
making
people
forget
their
troubles
simply
by
watching
them

*F*
*A*
*L*
*L.*

In a perfect world
a perfect place,

a place
where
you can be
absolutely
anything
you
possibly
want to be,

remember to
always ...

Be *YOURSELF!*

Look
at that face
in the mirror

*YOU*

are fabulous,

*YOU*

are beautiful,

So
pinch
those cheeks
and
smile,

Because
that
perfect
someone
Is
awesome

*YOU!*

Welcome
to
our unique

*HOME*

where
everyone
who enters
is free
to be
themselves.

live                          tranquility

create

empower                  relax

unwind

rejuvenate

smile

shine

calm

rest

peacefulness

Make
your
dreams
for
tomorrow,

become
a
reality
today!

With
each
and
every

*DREAM*

brings
the
hope
for
an
incredible
tomorrow.

Under a
sky of
sparkling
stars,
the small girl
looked up
and
dreamt
of all the
wonderful
things
possible
in life,

as one star

*F*
*E*
*L*
*L.*

An
incredible
Life
can
be
yours
If
you're
willing
to
reach

*F*

*A*

*R*

enough
for
the
stars!

Have you ever
just looked
at stones
tossed and
scattered amongst
the ground?

So many
colors
and shapes
some sparkle
some shine
some black
and some white.

A perfect mix.

Search
for me
in the quiet
moments
between
peace and chaos.

And then ..

remember to,
just breathe.

In
the
middle
of
all
this

*C*
*H*
*A*
*O*
*S*

and
confusion,

may
we
all
find
our
happy
medium.

May
gifts
from
above
be
showered

*D*
*O*
*W*
*N*

upon
you.

After
the storm
has ended,

Dance
barefoot
in the puddles.

The best things in life are ...

Family
 to
Love

Friends
 to
Make,

Places
 to
Go

and

Memories
 to
Treasure

Along
 the
Way.

If i were to die
tomorrow
what would you
remember
most about me.

Would you
remember
the size of
my bank account.

Would you
remember
the latest model
of car I drove.

Or would you
remember
the kindness
I shared with
all        who        knew        me.

I was always
attracted to
the bad boy type.

The kind
of boy that
my father hated
the kind
of boy that
kept a spare
cigarette tucked
behind his ear
and whiskey
in his glove box.

It took a few
bad boy
salty kisses
and
broken hearts
to realize
there's way more
to a good man
than his
bad boy looks.

Look deeper
love                                        stronger.

If he says
I'm not sure
how i feel
about you.

Kick him
to the curb
right away.

If it's
true love
he with know
how it feels
to                                                love.

Beware …

you are about
to enter
the home of a
published-author.

What happens
next ...
might just be
my future hit
storyline!

Proceed with caution ...

"chomp"

"chomp"

"chomp"

Is all I heard as
he chewed his food
above the racket
of the t.v. blaring ...

"thank-you"

You totally
motivated me
to take a
much needed
break
from writing
and get outside
with golden
sun shining
down.

- reap the rewards.

You are ...
brave
enough
to say
good-bye
to a life
of constant pain.

You are ...
strong
enough
to start
out fresh
in a life
of happiness.

You are
so much
more than ...

*ENOUGH!*

To truly
love someone
is
the greatest
gift
to ever be
given.

A special
gift
that can
never be
taken
away
or                                            replaced.

Love all of you ...

YOU          YOU                  YOU

                              YOU
YOU

                    YOU          YOU

YOU                    YOU

              YOU

                              YOU
YOU

              YOU        YOU

YOU
                    YOU

YOU                        YOU

          YOU
                    YOU    YOU

YOU                            YOU

She dreamt of
sun kissed skin
sand on her toes
and hair blowing
wildly in the breeze
as aqua waves
caress the shore
softly,

whispering her name.

This way
to the beach
where …

Flip flops
get tossed
In the sand
and best
memories
are made
in the sun!

My

*HAPPY*
*PLACE*

is
anywhere
as
long
as
I'm
with
you!

Never let
angry people
ruin your day.

Shake them off
like an old coat

And keep
right on

*SMILING!*

*YOU*

are
my
favourite
part
of
the
day!

Let me
get lost
and
forgotten
inside
the
solace
of
your wildest
dreams.

My mind
is now
truly open
to receiving
signs
from a
higher power
hidden
within
the beauty of
a dragonfly.

I imagine …

Years ago this house
was once full of life.

I imagine …

They square danced
in long ball gowns
to fiddle music playing
on the old a.m. radio
the smell of apple pie
and fresh buns baked
in the old cook stove.

- If these walls could talk.

When
you write
whatever
comes
to mind
as if
no one else
will ever
read it,
that is when
your true
masterpieces
will be
created.

Just leave me
locked away
inside an
empty room
with only
a pen and paper
and I'm sure …

I'll be just fine.

A good
book
can take you
to far away
places
you have
only
dreamed of.

He loves
all of me
scars and flaws
included,

I am one …

Lucky woman.

She dreamt
of conquering all
demons standing
in her way,

And so she did!

The perfect
story ...

Takes a lifetime
to write.

## ABOUT THE AUTHOR

Sin Dee is a Humber College Creative Writing graduate. She began scribbling in journals at a young age and now her work can be found in many online publications including Eye on Life, The Camel Saloon, and Route 7 online journals, among others. She has also published three poetry books entitled "Reminiscence," "Midnight Skies" and "As One Teardrop Falls," as well as a Memoir entitled "Signs from Beyond, a Spiritual Journey" all available for purchase on Amazon.

Please enjoy her latest collection of inspirational poetry, "Midnight Solace."

Other books by Sin Dee include:

Reminiscence, a book of poetry

Midnight Skies, a book of poetry

As One Teardrop Falls, a book of poetry

Signs From Beyond, a spiritual memoir

Autumn Breeze, a book of autumn poetry

Tis The Season, a collection of holiday poems

If you made it this far, it means that you must have finished the book!

Thank you so much for your interest in reading my work. It means the world to me!

Please remember to kindly leave me a review on Amazon. It is reviews from kind people like yourself that allows new authors to promote the sale of their books.

For more about the author, please follow her on Instagram at *author_sin_dee* for the latest poems and up to date information.

## MIDNIGHT SOLACE

A collection of inspirational poetry written by Sin Dee, author of Midnight Skies, Reminiscence and As One Teardrop Falls. In this fourth collection of poems, Dee takes us on a poetic journey of raw emotions as her poetry touches on recovery of toxic relationships, to heartache, breakups, and death as well as some uplifting motivational poetry to help you get over it and move on with your head held high!

*... this life we live is a beautiful place to be.*

*... spread your wings and venture all there is to see!*

Made in the USA
Columbia, SC
19 July 2024